"THE ACADEMY OF WARRE": MILITARY AFFAIRS IN IRELAND, 1600 TO 1800

The 30th O'Donnell Lecture

delivered by

Thomas Bartlett PhD MRIA

at
The Industry Centre, University College Dublin -
National University of Ireland, Dublin

on

Tuesday, 21 May 2002

€10

Ollscoil na hÉireann - National University of Ireland,
Tel: (353) 1 439 2424; **Fax:** (353) 1 439 2477;
Email: registrar@nui.ie

O'Donnell Lecture 2002 (30th lecture in the series)

"THE ACADEMY OF WARRE": MILITARY AFFAIRS IN IRELAND, 1600 TO 1800

Design and layout by Red Dog Design Consultants, Dublin 2
Printed by Elo Press Ltd., Dublin 8

ISSN: 1393-9726

ISBN: 0-901510-49-1

Price: €10

A DISCOURSE
OF
MILITARY
DISCIPLINE,

DEVIDED INTO

THREE BOOCKES,

DECLARINGE

The partes and fufficiencie ordained in a private Souldier, and in each Officer;

Servinge in the Infantery, till the election and office of the Captaine generall;

AND THE LASTE BOOKE TREATINGE OF
Fire-wourckes of rare executiones by fea and lande, as alfoe
of firtifafions.

Compofed by Captaine GERAT BARRY *Irish.*

AT BRUXELLS,
By the Widovve of Jhon Mommart.
M. DC. XXXIV.

Title page of Gerat Barry's *Discourse of Military Discipline* (Brussel's 1634).
Courtesy of the National Library of Ireland

Creative spelling is presumably attributable to a non-English speaking printer.

O'Donnell Lectures

Charles James O'Donnell, born 1850, provided a bequest in 1935 to fund an annual lecture in the National University of Ireland on the history of Ireland since the time of Cromwell, with particular reference to the histories, since 1641, of old Irish families.

The lecture series was established in 1957 and continued more or less annually until 1986. Due to lack of funds there was a gap of some years, but the NUI Senate was pleased to be able to revive the series in 1998. It was decided that a lecture would be presented annually from 1999 onwards, in rotation, in each of the NUI Constituent Universities.

The O'Donnell Lecture 1999 - *The urban patriciates of early modern Ireland: a case-study of Limerick* - was the first in the revived series and the 28th lecture overall. It was delivered by Colm Lennon at Callan Hall, National University of Ireland, Maynooth in November 1999 and has been published.

The 29th lecture in the series was delivered by Professor J.J. Lee in University College Cork - National University of Ireland Cork in February 2001: *Perspectives on the Irish Diaspora.*

Lectures in this series are now published with funds from the NUI Publications Scheme. The full list of O'Donnell Lectures is included on page 27.

Thomas Bartlett

Thomas Bartlett is a graduate of Queen's University, Belfast, where he completed his PhD in 1976. After lecturing in History at NUI Galway, he became Professor of Modern Irish History in University College Dublin in 1995.

Among his publications are *The Fall and Rise of the Irish Nation: The Catholic Question 1690 to 1830* (Dublin 1992), (with Keith Jeffery), *A Military History of Ireland* (Cambridge 1996), and an edition of *WTW Tone's Life of Theobald Wolfe Tone* (Dublin 1998). Professor Bartlett was awarded a Government of Ireland Senior Research Fellowship for the academic year 2002/03. He is a member of the Royal Irish Academy.

"THE ACADEMY OF WARRE": MILITARY AFFAIRS IN IRELAND, 1600 TO 1800[1]

Until recently, Irish warfare or indeed general military affairs in Ireland in the early modern period have not held the attention of the Irish historian. Admittedly, the pioneering work of Gerard Hayes-McCoy and Cyril Falls, and the substantial and on-going contributions by numerous authors in the journal *The Irish Sword* stand as a rebuke to this sweeping generalisation.[2] And latterly there are welcome signs that proper recognition is being accorded the importance of war in the shaping of modern Ireland.[3] None the less, it has remained true that historians of Ireland have by and large focussed, first, on the epic story of plantation, and its concomitants - anglicization and evangelisation - and then on the intricacies of Anglo-Irish economic, political and constitutional relations through the seventeenth and on into the long eighteenth centuries.[4] Moreover, if historians of Ireland - with notable exceptions - have tended to marginalise such subjects as the impact of war and the Irish military experience in the early modern period, those historians whose scholarly lives were, and are, devoted to military affairs in the Atlantic world, and on the European continent, have rarely seen fit to bring the Irish experience into the reckoning: until recently there was an almost entire absence of Ireland from the scholarly debate on the 'Military Revolution'.[5]

---

1   So Ireland was described by Colonel Laurence Crawford in *Ireland's ingratitude ... or a remonstrance of Colonel Crawford shewing the Jeuitical [sic] plots against the the parliament* (London, 1643) p.13: Cambridge University Library, Bradshaw collection [hereafter CUL, BC], Hib. 7.643.9

2   G.A.Hayes-McCoy, *Scots mercenary forces in Ireland, 1565-1603* (Dublin and London 1937); idem, *Irish battles* (London, 1969). Hayes-McCoy was for many years editor of *The Irish Sword* (Dublin, 1949-). Cyril Falls, *Elizabeth's Irish wars* (London, 1950); idem., *Mountjoy: Elizabethan general* (London, 1955). J.G.Simms' various articles on Irish military affairs are collected in D.Hayton and G.O'Brien (ed), *War and politics in Ireland 1649-1730* (London, 1987).

3   See especially Padraic Lenihan, *Confederate Catholics at war, 1641-49* (Cork, 2001); idem (ed), *Conquest and resistance: war in seventeenth-century Ireland* (Leiden, 2001); James S. Wheeler, *Cromwell in Ireland* (Dublin, 1999); Thomas Bartlett and Keith Jeffery (ed), *A Military History of Ireland* (Cambridge, 1996). M.C. Fissel, *English warfare 1511-1642* (London, 2001) has much to say about Ireland.

4   Neither of the two volumes in the *New History of Ireland* (Oxford, 1975, 1984) dealing with the period 1534 to 1801 has any chapter on Irish military matters.

5   See now Geoffrey Parker and Rolf Loeber, 'The military revolution in seventeenth-century Ireland' in Jane Ohlmeyer (ed), *Ireland: from independence to occupation, 1641-1660* (Cambridge, 1995), pp. 66-88; and Bruce Lenman's two-volume study, *England's colonial wars, 1550-1688*, and *Britain's colonial wars, 1688-1783* (London, 2001)

Perhaps the reason for this neglect lies in the perception that warfare in Ireland was so irredeemably primitive as scarcely to allow the designation of 'war'?[6] The 'Celtic Way of War' - the customary designation accorded Irish military tactics - stressed the Irish facility with ambushes and skirmishes, with raids being carried out, as an observer in the 1640s dismissively put it, by 'this running campe of rebels [who] doe scatter themselves up and down the country'.[7] Irish warfare was characterised by an innate Irish propensity to stay in or near woods and bogs (one English commander referred scornfully to what he called the Irish soldiers' 'best fort, a bogge')[8], to shun plains or open ground and, above all, an especial mark of ignominy, to avoid battle. And when battle was joined, the sole Irish tactic was held to be the Highland charge, a headlong rush with sword and buckler, with little trace of that close coordination between horse and foot that allegedly distinguished military engagements on other battlefields. Moreover the numbing ferocity with which Irish wars were conducted, at least from the 1560s to the 1650s, but with unmistakable echoes in the 1790s, the perceived lack of importance (and frequency) of Irish battles and wars *in a European context*, and even the apparent limited size of the forces engaged in them, have combined to set them apart from what might be called professional or sophisticated warfare on the European continent. Certainly, just as modern military historians have by and large ignored Ireland, so too seventeenth-century military theorists saw no need to include this country in their works. The Earl of Cork's son, Lord Orrery, certainly played a vital role in the wars of the Confederation, but yet in his *A Treatise of the Art of War* (London, 1677), Ireland is barely mentioned: nor did his county compatriot, the Cork-born Gerat Barry in his *A Discourse of Military Discipline* (Brussels, 1634) see fit to draw on Irish military experience for purposes of illustration.[9] Perhaps Barnaby Rich, a less elevated observer, though one who by his own admission was 'a professed soldier' with many years of soldiering in Ireland, put his finger on the problem. In his *A New Description of Ireland* (London, 1610) he was robustly dismissive of the Irish military experience. Vexed by a throwaway remark from the Old English writer Richard Stanihurst to the effect that, among other laudable qualities, the Irish were 'delighted with warres', Rich 'unrip'd' (his own word) a scathing rebuke: 'No! they are delighted with rebellions,... tumults, discentions,

---

6   See,James Michael Hill, *Celtic warfare, 1595-1763* (Edinburgh, 1986); and for a critique of Hill's thesis see Padraic Lenihan, '"Celtic warfare" in the 1640s' in John R. Young (ed), *Celtic dimensions of the British civil wars* (Edinburgh, 1997, pp. 116-40). See also Grady McWhiney and Perry D. Anderson, *Attack and die: civil war military tactics and the southern heritage* (Alabama, 1982) which argues that adherence to the tactics of 'celtic warfare' led to the battlefield defeat of the Confederate army in 1865.

7   *A wild-fire plot found out in Ireland: shewing how the rebels would have consumed ... Dublin ... Also how three lords were taken prisoners ... and the Scots ... joyned battle ...* (London, 6641 [sic]): CUL, BC Hib. 7.641.117

8   *A Iournall of the most memorable passages in Ireland. Especially ... at Munster, beginning the 26. of August 1642 ... written by a worthy gentleman who was present* (London, 1642): CUL, BC Hib. 7.642.48

9   Copies of both of these volumes are available in the National Library of Ireland.

uprores, ... commotions and insurrections ... ; but they cannot be called wars that are stirred up by subjects against their Prince ... .' In any case, he continued loftily, '[the Irish] are altogether unfurnished of all manner of warlike necessaries either for defence or offence, neither are they able so to fortifie themselves in any ground of advantage but that men are still able to fetch them out by the eares either by force or by engine; they cannot deal so with the English for they having neither artillerie to batter nor means to approach, a small company of our English soldiers will make good any place against the whole forces of the Irish... .'[10]

And yet, despite the strictures of Barnaby Rich, and notwithstanding the apparent lack of interest by Barry and Orrery, there is a strong case to be made for viewing military affairs in Ireland in the early modern period as quite central to the Irish historical experience, even to the emergence of an Irish identity. It is not just that according to the theorists of colonisation, a successful plantation in Ireland could only be set in train following military conquest; nor is it that that military conquest, it is now clear, involved far larger sums of money, numbers of men and amounts of matèriel than had been hitherto acknowledged. These are self-evidently important, with implications for the uneven progress of plantations and for their later character. Equally, such considerations had serious consequences for the development of government in Ireland, because with a military establishment running at between three and twenty times the cost of the civil establishment in the period 1600 to 1800, one could be forgiven for seeing Irish government as little more than a revenue wing - a sort of civil commissariat - of the army in Ireland.[11] More than these, however, the way that a society conducts warfare tell us much about that society - its values, its ethos, even, perhaps especially, its self-definition. Lastly, a consideration of military matters in Ireland may shed light on the vexed question of Ireland's ambiguous position within the wider Atlantic world - an issue that currently divides both literary critics and historians. Ireland was undoubtedly part of the Stuart and Hanoverian composite monarchy; she constituted an integral element of the British archipelago, and had close aristocratic connections to the elites of Scotland and England (and strong military ties to continental Europe). But there was, none the less, a strong whiff of the frontier and of the colonial about Ireland in the early modern period. Can we situate Irish warfare and the Irish wars between what might be called the sophisticated warfare of continental Europe, where conflicts were conducted by battles and sieges, with regular and orderly manoeuvres, even with rudimentary laws of war in force (if not always enforced)? Or must we look to the colonial model, where wars were conducted with relatively small numbers of combatants, where the enemy was portrayed as inhuman,

10 Barnaby Rich, *A new description of Ireland* (London, 1610): CUL, BC Hib. 7.61.2, p. 9

11 See the figures for the military establishments in the large manuscript volume entitled *Militarium*. National Archives, Dublin, M999/308/3. I am indebted to my colleague Dr Ivar McGrath for guidance on the cost of the civil estabishment over this period.

unchristian, barbarous and savage, and where the sole object of the ferocious campaigns was the utter destruction or extirpation of the foe?[12] We may remember that while France, or the Netherlands or even the English might lose the odd war, these countries could and did recover; for the Aztec and the Inca - and for the Algonquin Indians of New England, and the native Irish, however, there would be no way back: they lost and faded from view. Is Irish warfare to be seen as european or colonial; do we locate the 'Academy of Warre' within the kingdom or the colony?

We may begin our discussion with what historians have chosen to designate 'the military revolution'. The concept is a recent one; its genesis can be dated quite precisely to the occasion of the inaugural lecture delivered by Michael Roberts before the Queen's University of Belfast on 21 January 1955 on his appointment to the chair of modern history in that institution. Now, to paraphrase Jane Austen, it is a melancholy truth universally acknowledged that most inaugural lectures delivered by newly-appointed professors by and large fall dead-born from the press; a cause of some concern to the university's appointments board, and of some considerable consolation to the incumbent's unsuccessful rivals. Some professorial reputations, it may be said, never wholly recover from the inaugural lecture. But such was emphatically not the fate with Roberts' lecture, 'The Military Revolution, 1560-1660'.[13] It was not just Roberts' sonorous, yet stirring prose style - who could nowadays use correctly the adverb 'infrangibly'?- nor his linguistic dexterity - sources in no fewer than nine languages (not including English) were cited - nor even the ostensible subject matter of his talk - an early modern revolution in things military, however striking this idea might be - that commanded the rapt attention of his audience at the time. These were all, of course, important; but what has ensured near permanent discussion, argument, refinement, and attempted rebuttal of Roberts' arguments over the next fifty years was his central conclusion which explicitly traced the origins of twentieth-century warfare to a date in the seventeenth century. He wrote:

> By 1660 the modern art of war had come to birth. Mass armies, strict discipline, the control of the state, the submergence of the individual had already arrived: the conjoint ascendancy of financial power and applied science was already established in all its malignity; the use of propaganda, psychological warfare, and terrorism as military weapons were already familiar to theorists, as well as to commanders in the field.

12 There is a voluminous literature on warfare in the British colonies of north America: particularly germane to this essay are Jill Lepore, *The Name of War: King Phillips war and the origins of American identity* (New York, 1998); P.M. Malone, *The skulking way of war: technology and tactics among the New England Indians* (New York, 1991); Armstrong Starkey, *European and native American warfare, 1675-1815* (London, 1998); and Lenman, *Colonial wars*, op. cit

13 Roberts' essay has been many times reprinted. It is conveniently available in Clifford J. Rogers, *The military revolution debate: readings on the military transformation of early modern Europe* (Colorado and Oxford, 1999), pp. 13-36

The last remaining qualms as to the religious and ethical legitimacy of
war seemed to have been stilled. The road lay open, broad and straight,
to the abyss of the twentieth century.

In his analysis of this military revolution which took place in the period, 1560-
1660, Roberts placed special weight on four developments. First, in place of dense
crowds of pikemen hurling themselves at each other, he stressed the emergence of
the linear formation of smaller, uniform units firing salvos at each other, usually in
combination with charging cavalry and well-directed artillery. Such tactics demanded
a much higher degree than hitherto thought requisite of training and discipline along
with an emphasis on uniform dress and marching in step. And these in their turn
cost money, so much so that governments were reluctant to disband such trained
soldiers and they began to be retained on a permanent basis - the origin of standing
armies. Second, Roberts emphasised what he called 'a revolution in strategy', which
might involve the deployment of several armies in the one theatre and which would
seek to destroy the enemy's army in a decisive battle. Gustavus Adolphus had
several armies on the go in Germany in the early 1630s, and he destroyed Tilly's army
at the battle of Breitenfeld in 1631. Next, Roberts identified a prodigious increase in
the manpower - especially musketeers - deployed to fight wars: Philipp II of Spain
made do with 40,000 troops in the late sixteenth century; a hundred years later, Louis
XIV fielded some 400,000; while a further hundred years on, Bonaparte had nearly a
million men at his disposal. Lastly, and clearly related to the preceding, Roberts
pointed to the new destructiveness of war and the new costliness of war, both
developments which posed major problems for early modern rulers, their
governments and their respective civilian populations. Paying for these new armies,
clothing them and feeding them, made necessary intrusive commissariats and new
bureaucracies, and these in their turn reinforced the trend, as he saw it, towards
absolutism. Admittedly, Roberts also pointed to the decline of mercenaries, the
attempts made to formulate laws to govern warfare during this period and the
political and constitutional repercussions of the 'military revolution' he was describing:
but he did so only in passing, and these four developments in tactics, strategy,
manpower, and administration constituted for him the essential 'military revolution'.

Roberts' thesis won immediate and general acceptance, being endorsed by Sir
George Clark in his *War and Society in the Seventeenth Century* (Cambridge, 1958)
and in his chapter in the *New Cambridge Modern History* (1964). It was to be a
further ten years before a serious criticism was mounted, that by Geoffrey Parker in
his '"The Military Revolution" 1560-1660; a myth?',[14] and Parker elaborated on his
critique a decade later in *The Military Revolution: Military Innovation and the Rise of
the West* (Cambridge, 1986). Further questioning of Roberts' thesis came from

---

14 Reprinted in Rogers (ed) *Military revolution debate*, pp. 37-54

eighteenth-century historians such as Jeremy Black and from sixteenth-century historians such as Thomas Arnold.[15] Medieval historians, too, soon uncovered their own 'military revolution' in the fourteenth century and the historians of technology were determined not to be left out of the debate.[16]

To date, criticism has focused chiefly on timing and on causation. Parker has dismissed the year 1560 as of no significance and he has instead traced the key developments to an earlier period, stressing the importance of the development between 1500 to 1520 of a new type of artillery fortress, the *Trace Italienne*.[17] This style of fortification began in Italy and consisted of 'a circuit of low thick walls punctuated by quadrilateral bastions' which returned the advantage to the defenders, and made a storm a highly risky business. Battles too became rarer: they decided little, were high-risk undertakings, had little part in strategy, and hence were best avoided.

Sieges and siege-warfare dominated strategy: as Lord Orrery put it in 1677 'Battels do not now decide national quarrels ... for we make war more like foxes than like lyons; and you will have twenty sieges for one battel'.[18] These new fortresses required large numbers of soldiers to defend and to besiege, and Parker saw this as a direct explanation for the great increase in manpower with which seventeenth-century wars were fought.

However, while Parker has argued cogently for an earlier date and even a reformulation of the 'military revolution' thesis, others have contended that Roberts' terminal date - 1660 - is equally unsatisfactory. Jeremy Black has focused on a much later period: contrary to what Roberts maintained, the year 1660 did not usher in an era of 'stagnation, indecisiveness and conservatism' in warfare. In fact, Black argues that the major changes in warfare took place after 1660, and he highlighted the growth of navies and improvements in naval organisation and technology (the broadside, for example), and the marked growth in the size of armies during the eighteenth century. The period post-1660 was that when European superiority over Asia and other non-European powers became decisive: and given that this superiority has remained to this day, Black's contention that the key period of military innovation was the eighteenth century is clearly worthy of attention.

---

15 Jeremy Black summarises his misgivings about the Roberts' thesis in Rogers (ed), *Military revolution debate*, pp. 95-116. See also Jeremy Black (ed), *European warfare, 1453-1815* (London, 1999), which contains Arnold's essay 'War in sixteenth-century Europe: revolution and renaissance', pp. 23-44

16 See Michael Prestwich, *Armies and warfare in the middle ages: the English experience* (New Haven, 1996): Conclusion, 'A military revolution?'; and John Guilmartin Jr's essay 'The military revolution: origins and first tests abroad' in Rogers (ed) *Military revolution debate*, pp. 299-336

17 See Parker's book-length reflections on this topic: Geoffrey Parker, *The Military Revolution: military innovation and the rise of the west, 1500-1800* (Cambridge, 1988).

18 Orrery, *Treatise of the art of war*, p. 15

Where does the military experience of Ireland stand in this debate? From my introduction it will come as no surprise that despite the fact that Roberts' inaugural lecture was composed, written, and delivered in Belfast, he made no reference to Irish wars, battles or sieges. And for the next forty years, the Irish experience of war did not feature in the scholarly debate on the military revolution. Only in the last few years have there been been encouraging signs that the Irish military experience in the early modern period may have something to offer the historian interested in the question of a military revolution or revolutions.

In the time available to me it would obviously be unwise to attempt a detailed treatment of the five wars of the period 1590 to 1800 - that is, the Nine Years War of 1594-1603; the Confederate Wars of the 1640s; the Cromwellian Campaigns in Ireland, 1649-53; the War of the Two Kings 1689-91; and lastly the Rebellion of 1798. However, some general points may be made, before offering a rather more detailed treatment of the wars of the1640s. I propose then to go on to identify an Irish military revolution in the eighteenth century which has no precise European parallels; and lastly to conclude with some reflections on war, society and identity in early modern Ireland.

From the work of historians such as Morgan[19], Ó hAnnracháin[20], Lenihan and Parker it is now clear that however we define the military revolution, and however we prioritise the various elements within it, Ireland and the Irish experience of war ought not to be neglected.

Morgan in his study of the O'Neill wars of the 1590s has shown how the new battlefield tactics were quickly imported into Ireland and adapted to Irish conditions. O'Neill's victory at Clontibret in 1595 revealed an alarming ability to combine shot and cavalry to good effect. A worried Irish council noted in its report that 'these traitors [i.e. O'Neill and his allies] are increased to a greater strength in numbers and wonderfully altered from their Irish manner of arms and the use thereof, besides their order and discipline in governing their men'.[21] O'Neill's victory at the battle of the Yellow Ford is well known but less so was his tactical withdrawal some years later when threatened by Lord Mountjoy. At the Moyry Pass near Newry, O'Neill drew up an impressive line of entrenchments - a labyrinth of walls, banks, pallisades, thorn abatis and drystone flanking works - which successfully delayed Mountjoy's forces for over a month. Mountjoy reported that in building such defences 'these barbarous people ... had far exceeded their custom and our expectation'.[22] Indeed, O'Neill's skilful deployment of his men posed a problem for those commentators for whom it

---

19 Hiram Morgan, *Tyrone's rebellion: the outbreak of the nine years war in Ireland* (London, 1993)

20 See Tadhg Ó hAnnracháin, *Catholic reformation in Ireland: the mission of Rinuccini, 1645-1649* (Oxford, 2002)

21 Cited Morgan, *Tyrone's rebellion*, p. 179

22 Cited Hayes-McCoy, *Irish battles*, p. 136

was axiomatic that the Irish could not naturally fight in a modern or manly, i.e. English way. For Barnaby Rich, and for Thomas Gainsford the solution had to lie in the assistance which O'Neill received from disaffected members of the English community in Ireland, and from his ruse of sending in rotation 500 recruits to Elizabeth's captains and thereby over time 'got most of his men to be able souldiers'.[23] It was this capacity for military innovation that made the 'Arch-rebell Tirone' so difficult and expensive to defeat, and that for fifty years after his death made his name a nightmare for English governors in Ireland.[24]

The military revolution was imported into Ireland chiefly through returning swordsmen. From an early date it was reported that the 1641 rebels 'expect some ayd, assistance, armes and supply from forainne countries, both from France and Spain', and within a few months of the outbreak of the rebellion there were reports of Spanish 'cullors' being borne by the rebels.[25] In 1640, there were some 1,300 Irish in the army of Spanish Flanders, and there was nearly as many in the French army: many, possibly most, of these veterans of wars in the Low Countries and elsewhere came back to Ireland in the early 1640s.[26]

Understandably, these returning soldiers were a cause of acute anxiety to those charged with suppressing the 1641 rebellion in Ireland; and in the final breakdown in relations between Charles and his parliament scarcely any charge weighed more heavily against him than that he had knowingly permitted Irish veterans - 'men bred in the wars in the service of the King of Spain' - to return to Ireland in the early months of 1642.[27] Parliamentary spokesmen forcibly reminded Charles that while the rebels in Ireland had abundant manpower, yet they were 'for the most part ignorant of the use of their arms [and] could by no means become dangerous or formidable to this kingdom but by the access of souldiers and commanders wherein they were like to be furnished out of France and Flanders'.[28] Equally, many of the Scottish and English soldiers who fought in Ireland in the 1640s had borne arms in the Thirty Years War. The Stewart brothers who commanded the Laggan Army in North-west Ulster had fought on the continent, the Scottish general Monro had served with no less a military innovator than Gustavus Adophus; and the elderly Sir Charles Coote, a fierce

23 Thomas Gainsford, *The true exemplary and remarkable history of the earl of Tirone* (London, 1619), p. 37: CUL, BC Hib. 7.61.16

24 So he is described in Emanuel van Meteren, *A true discourse historicall of the succeeding governors in the Netherlands and the civill wars begun there in the yeere 1565* (London, 1602): CUL, BC Hib. 7.60.1

25 *The Irish petition to this parliament in England* (London, 1641): CUL, BC 7.641.51; *A treacherous plot of a confederacie in Ireland ... sent over by Mr August, minister of Gods Wood in the county of Lymbricke* (London, 1641): CUL, BC 7.641.108

26 Parker and Loeb, 'Military revolution in seventeenth-century Ireland', p. 72; Ó hAnnracháin, 'The strategic involvement of continental powers in Ireland, 1596-1691' in Lenihan (ed), *Conquest and resistance*, pp. 25-52; David Parrot, *Richelieu's army: war, government and society in France, 1624-1642* (Cambridge, 2001)

27 *A message sent from both houses of parliament to the King's majesty ... concerning speciall matters* (London, 1642): CUL, BC Hib. 7.642.1/31

28 *The answer of both houses of parliament to the King's message* (London, 1642): CUL, BC Hib. 7.642.10

and resolute foe of Irish rebels in the 1640s, had a military career that stretched back to the 1590s when, as one account had it, he was 'trained in a military way' by that Elizabethan military legend, Sir John Norreys.[29] The expertise and experience of these veterans was greatly valued and they became, as it were, professors in the Irish 'Academy of Warre'. Evidence of their influence was soon visible. In January 1642, one observer reported how a rebel army appeared before Kinsale 'in passing good order as ever [I] saw rebels since I came over; his horse being at least four or five hundred compleatly armed with pike, musket or calliver'. The experience sufficiently unsettled the witness to lead him to 'suspect something, seeing that a rebel but lately risen and of no great note, this being the very first exploit that ever he took in hand ... should in so short a time be able to raise so many men and in that manner to furnish them'.[30] A year later, one commentator taunted those forces deployed against the Confederate Catholics that the day was over for slaughtering 'disarmed clownes ... weaponless and in no fit posture to defend themselves'.[31] And another reflecting on the rebels' defeat at the important battle of Liscarroll, County Cork, 1643 remarked with surprise that the rebels 'were not such as formerly we met, naked rogues, but brave and gallant men, armed as well as ourselves nor did they want anything but a good cause'.[32] It was however among what may be called the Scottish or royalist or parliamentary forces that the influence of the new warfare can most readily be seen. In particular, devastating volley fire from massed musketeers resolutely rotating from front to rear led to a string of very costly rebel defeats.

In one battle in County Cork, the rebels were routed when Sir Simon Harcourt's men were able 'in one whole body ... to powre in such a volley of shot into the rebels grosse that they dropped wonderfully';[33] in another, by 'discharging [their muskets] so continually quick that there was not space of the motion of the heart or the twinkling of an eye for an hour and a half altogether', the rebels were put to flight with very heavy casualties.[34] Of course, such sustained volleys of fire required training and drill of a high order; and that was not always available. At the vital battle of Julianstown in late 1641, the Ulster rebels won an important victory when an officer on the opposing side commanded his men to perform 'a counter-march in which

29 David Stevenson, *Scottish covenanters and Irish confederates* (Belfast, 1981), pp. 80-81: *A discourse concerning the rebellion in Ireland ... a commemoration of ... Sir Charles Coot deceased* (London, 1642): CUL, BC Hib. 5.542.2

30 *A true and good relation of the valliant exploits and victorious enterprises of Sir Simon Harcourt and Sir Charles Coote* (London, 1641/2): CUL, BC Hib. 7.641.11

31 *Querees, propounded by the Protestant party concerning the peace in general, now treated of in Ireland and the answers ... made in behalf and name of the Irish nation* (Paris, 1644): CUL, BC Hib. 7.644.31

32 *A iournall of the most memorable passages in Ireland. Especially ... at Munster ... wherein is ... the siege of Ardmore Castle... with ... Liscarroll* (London, 1642): CUL, BC Hib. 7.642.48

33 *A true and good relation of the valliant exploits and victorious enterprises of Sir Simon Harcourt and Sir Charles Coote*, op.cit.

34 *A true and perfect diurnall of the most remarkable passages in Ireland...* (London, 1642): CUL, BC Hib. 7.642.102

they being compelled to take a ditch' became confused and disordered, and 'the [rebels] judging it a flight gave such a shout that frighted them into a further confusion and so presently charging them' carried the day.[35] Perhaps the most obvious example of the new warfare was at the battle of Benburb in 1646, a great victory won by Owen Roe O'Neill and the Army of Ulster. This has been described as a victory by a Spanish-trained general, employing 'the classic defensive techniques favoured by the Habsburgs', over Robert Munro, a Gustavus Adolphus-trained general.[36] In fact, Owen Roe O'Neill's cavalry got the better of Monro's and as Monro's horse fell back into the ranks of the packed footsoldiers huge confusion ensued, gifting victory to the Ulster Army. And yet, like most of the relatively few battles in the Thirty Years War, Benburb achieved little: O'Neill chose not to pursue Monro and instead hastened to Kilkenny to make political capital out of his victory.[37]

In other areas of the military campaigns of the 1640s, the impact of the new doctrines can be seen. There had been extensive construction of the artillery fortress (or something like it) in Ireland in the seventeenth century (forts at Kinsale, Cork, Galway, Dunluce, Smerwick, Charlemont and Derry were all constructed or reinforced in the early years of the century)[38] and this was entirely comparable with the contemporary european experience, and so too was the resultant emphasis on siege warfare in the various campaigns of the later seventeenth century. In 1689, the failure of James II's army to take Derry following a protracted (and incompetent) siege clearly signalled the collapse of the Jacobite armies in the field the following year. Examining the record for the 1640s, Lenihan remarks that the Confederates 'enthusiastically embraced the contemporaneous military revolution in so far as it related to siegecraft and fortifications',[39] and this verdict has been endorsed by Loeber and Parker: Ireland in the 1640s was 'no less rapid and no less impressive' than England in taking up the new ways of war.[40]

An Irish officer in the Spanish service, Gerat Barry, had published a *Discourse of Military Discipline* at Brussels in 1634 - probably the first military manual from the pen of an Irish author - and in the third section he had an up-to-date and well-illustrated discussion of fortifications. But even before the 1630s the

35 Nicholas Bernard, *The whole proceedings of the siege of Drogheda in Ireland* ... (London, 1642): CUL, Hib. 7.642.14

36 Parker and Loeb, 'Military revolution in seventeenth-century Ireland', p. 73

37 J.C. Beckett, 'The confederation of Kilkenny reviewed' in *Confrontations: studies in Irish history* (London, 1972), pp. 61-2. But see also Padraic Lenihan, 'Confederate military strategy' in Michael O Siochrú (ed) *Kingdoms in crisis: Ireland in the 1640s* (Dublin, 2001), pp. 166-7

38 P.M.Kerrigan, *Castles and fortifications in Ireland, 1485-1945* (Cork, 1995), chpt. 3

39 Lenihan, 'Celtic warfare in the 1640s', p. 125; see also Lenihan, 'Ireland's military revolutions' in Lenihan (ed), *Conquest and resistance*, pp. 345-9

40 Parker and Loeb, 'Military revolution in seventeenth-century Ireland', p. 88

importance of siege-warfare was evident. It was in essence Mountjoy's successful siege of Kinsale in which O'Neill's Spanish allies were installed that marked a decisive turning-point in the Nine Years' War.[41] Indeed, the noted military historian Christopher Duffy has claimed that 'The siege of Kinsale deserves to be numbered among the decisive contests of history ... it bears comparison with the victories of Cortes and Pizarro in the New World: like those actions, it signified the end of an ancient order of things'.[42] As in other areas of military endeavour, returning Irish swordsmen from the continent brought with them much valuable experience of siege warfare. The Preston brothers had saved Louvain for the Spanish in 1635, while their great rival Owen Roe O'Neill had defended Arras: they were all to return to take up command positions during the Confederate wars; though it may be argued that battles were not their forte.[43] And, as is well-known, Cromwell's progress in Ireland in 1649-50 was marked by a series of storms of defended royalist towns: some successful (and notorious) - the sacks of Drogheda and of Wexford - others less so, those of Limerick and of Clonmel.[44] Cromwell's attempted storm of Clonmel may in fact be seen as the gravest setback to his military career. The town was defended by a confederate army under Hugh Dubh O'Neill, a veteran of the Spanish wars, who set a simple trap for Cromwell's hitherto victorious Ironsides. O'Neill permitted Cromwell's men to enter the town through a breach in the walls. O'Neill had had built lengthy walls with firing positions on each side of the breach and he positioned artillery pieces at the far end of the walls. Unusually, O'Neill's men practised the countermarch, by which each man fired his musket and then retired to the rear enabling another to take his place while they reloaded. As a result the attackers gained no respite from the musket volleys: O'Neill's artillery completed the rout by firing chainshot into the densely packed parliamentarians. Cromwell's impetuosity or his lack of experience in siege warfare, or both, may have cost him as many as 2000 casualties; and he only took Clonmel when he agreed terms to allow the defenders, having exhausted their ammunition, to march out unharmed.[45]

In general, however, for all their experience in siege warfare, the Confederate commanders and their armies of the 1640s had little success in taking the towns or castles to which the British had fled after the rebellion, and they had as little success in defending those forts and castles they did possess. Their failure in this respect

---

41 J.J. Silke, *Kinsale: the Spanish intervention in Ireland at the end of the Elizabethan wars* (Liverpool, 1970)

42 C. Duffy, *Siege warfare: the fortress in the early modern world* (New York, 1979), p. 145

43 For the pre-1641 careers of, and rivalry between, Owen Roe O'Neill and Thomas Preston see Jerrold I. Casway, *Owen Roe O'Neill and the struggle for Catholic Ireland* (Pennsylvania, 1984); Lenihan, 'Ireland's military revolutions', p. 353

44 James Scott Wheeler, *Cromwell in Ireland* (Dublin, 1999)

45 See James Burke, 'Siege warfare in seventeenth-century Ireland' in Lenihan (ed), *Conquest and resistance*, pp. 257-91

and, indeed, their near total battlefield failure may be attributed to their critical shortage of gunpowder and arms - O'Neill's exploits at Clonmel were almost unique - and, to a lesser extent, to their inadequate horse.

Gerat Barry, Confederate general in Munster, commanded the mining that led to the surrender of King John's fort in Limerick and the Confederates also captured the Parliamentarian fort at Duncannon.[46] But these were rare examples of successful sieges by them. More typical was the rebels' failure to take Drogheda having besieged it for five months; on the other hand, the rebel town of Dundalk which the rebels had 'to their uttermost fortified' fell in one day to an assault by government forces.[47] Without adequate supplies of powder and weapons, the Confederate regiments could not practice the countermarch, and hence were almost always out-gunned on the field. When at one battle or skirmish in 1642, the rebels lost some 140 muskets, it was claimed in Dublin that this was 'more loss to them, by report, than three thousand men, so few they have of arms';[48] and at the siege of Drogheda (1642-3), the defenders taunted the Confederate attackers with their lack of powder, 'offering to throw them a bag if they would but fetch it'. (The background to this story is that the rebel commander, Sir Phelim O'Neill, had sought unsuccessfully both to impress his own men and overawe the garrison by colouring barrels of sand to look like gunpowder: humiliatingly, the deception failed).[49]

It was a similar story with artillery: the Confederates well appreciated its importance and they undertook desperate efforts to redress their supplies of cannon and gunpowder. There are some suggestions that they set up their own iron foundries; they certainly removed cannon from ships seized and forts captured, and they received some quantity of munitions from abroad. What held back the Confederates from developing a substantial artillery was not an attachment to the highland charge or an aversion to military innovation but rather an acute shortage of powder. Nor was inventiveness any substitute for the real thing: at one siege in Cavan the rebels brought up a 'great [artillery] piece on carriages' with which to overawe the besieged garrison and to intimidate them into making terms. The tactic failed however when the rebels' bluff was called, for it was quickly revealed that their so-called great cannon, as was reported 'could not speak for itself being counterfeit and made of wood'.[50] (Forty years later in the Jacobite war, a similar bluff failed when at Enniskillen the Jacobite besiegers brought up a siege gun hauled by eight

46 See Kenneth Wiggins, Anatomy of a siege: King John's castle, Limerick, 1642 (Bray, Co. Wicklow, 2000), p. 222; Lenihan, 'Ireland's military revolutions', p. 353

47 Bernard, *The whole proceedings of the siege of Drogheda in Ireland ...* op.cit.

48 *Good newes from Ireland, from Kimsale, Bandum, Clarakelty* [sic] ... (London, 1642): CUL, BC, Hib. 7.642.47

49 Bernard, *The whole proceedings of the siege of Drogheda in Ireland ...* op. cit.

50 Henry Jones, *A remonstrance of the rebellion in Cavan, within Ulster... from 23 October 1641 untill the 15 of June 1642* (London, 1642): CUL, BC Hib. 7.642.95

horses. A quick sally by a party of the besieged garrison revealed that the cannon was in fact 'a tin gun covered with leather': one of the beseiged brought it on his shoulder back to the town.[51])

This lack of gunpowder, and an inadequate supply of muskets as much as adherence to Spanish military theory (which downplayed the importance of battles) may explain why the Confederate commanders were reluctant to be drawn into set-piece battles, why they 'did not dare to oppose our men but runne away and gaze afar off, deere-like'.[52]

In other respects, too, Ireland's military experience in the seventeenth century appears to be comparable to other countries in Europe. Appreciating the importance of naval power, the Confederate Catholics had a small squadron of privateers which operated out of Wexford and this caused parliament much disproportionate anxiety.[53] It was a desire to root out these armed merchantmen that led Cromwell to advance so directly on Wexford after the fall of Drogheda. Moreover, recent work on army size indicates that the Confederates were able to maintain armies of around 20,000 men; and this has been computed at about 1.3% of the available males. This percentage is about half that mobilised by the English parliament but given the much smaller fiscal base of the confederate government this was still a considerable force of men. In the 1640s, the Scots fielded an army of 16,000 in Ulster, largely in Antrim and Down, but inadequate arrangements to feed and pay them curbed their effectiveness: given the deficient logistics, a debacle like Benburb might have been foreseen.[54] Similarly large armies of up to 30,000 men were deployed during the Williamite Wars. The point here is that, in Ireland as elsewhere, the huge efforts to maintain large armies in the field had a direct impact on state organisation and power.

'War made the state and the state made war': Charles Tilly's aphorism has a clear relevance for Ireland, for it might be argued that the Irish state in the seventeenth and eighteenth centuries largely existed to keep up a large military force.[55] After 1699, Ireland maintained a standing army of (officially) 12,000 men (after 1769, 15,500 men) and while this was ostensibly deployed to defend Ireland from external and internal

---

51 *A true and impartial account of the most material passages in Ireland since December 1688* ... (London, 1689): CUL, BC Hib. 7.689.13. Harman Murtagh has argued that this was not in fact a 'mock' cannon but rather a poorly constructed real one. H. Murtagh, 'Unusual artillery at the siege of Crom Castle, 1689', in *Irish Sword*, vol. xviii (no. 70), pp. 81-82

52 *A true relation of the proceedings of the Scottish armie now in Ireland, by three letters* ... (London, 1642): CUL, BC Hib.7.642.1/11

53 Lenihan, *Confederate Catholics at war*, p. 177

54 Ibid., chapter 2

55 For the importance of the armed forces and waging war in state formation see John Brewer, *The sinews of power: war, money and the English state* (London, 1989); Michael J. Braddick, *State formation in early modern England, 1550-1770* (Cambridge, 2000); James Scott Wheeler, *The making of a world power: war and the military revolution in seventeenth-century England* (Stroud, Gloucs., 1999)

enemies, it was in fact a convenient way for ministers to circumvent the long-standing English suspicion of standing armies on English soil. There was in fact a large English standing army; but most of it was kept in Ireland, and paid for by Ireland, out of sight of prying parliamentary eyes.[56] If that army had been removed from the Irish establishment, it would have been difficult to justify the continued existence of the Irish state apparatus for so much of it was designed to pay, clothe, feed and administer the Irish military establishment. Throughout the eighteenth century a very large proportion of Irish government expenditure went on the upkeep of the armed forces in Ireland. And in the 1790s, when the Irish state bankrupted itself under the pressure of war - when it could no longer make war - it offered an opportunity to two groups who sought radical change: the United Irishmen who wanted Ireland to be a satellite republic of France, and British ministers who had long desired to get rid of the Irish parliament.

In these ways, then, the Irish experience of war and warfare in the period 1600 to 1800 seems to fit in well with the wider European perspective. The new tactics were embraced in Ireland on all sides, the importance of artillery fortresses was recognised at an early date, siege warfare dominated over battles, an appropriate administration was constructed by which to 'feed Mars', and towards the end of our period there was a substantial growth in the Irish army. Something which may appropriately be designated an Irish military revolution would seem to have taken place between 1600 and 1800.

However, there was a further key development in the military history of Ireland during this period, one that may properly be described as revolutionary. This was the progressive recruitment of Irish Catholics to the ranks of the armed forces of the crown; a process that was concentrated into the last thirty years of the eighteenth century. To appreciate the revolutionary nature of this change one need only recall the deeply suspicious attitude of the British observers towards Irish soldiers in the 1590s when O'Neill's triumphs were partly attributed to the number of Irish serving in Bagenal's and Mountjoy's army. Admittedly in 1643, one parliamentary pamphleteer had reminded his audience that the Roman custom had been to 'incorporate those whom they conquered', that from their colonies 'the greatest part of their armies was ... raised' and that 'we can find another England in Ireland'.[57] But such sentiments were cast aside: throughout the 1640s, Irish soldiers captured by the enemy were regularly killed out of hand: we may note *inter alia* the 300 soldiers put to the sword by Inchiquin's men at Callan, county Kilkenny in 1647; the slaughter of the garrison of 200 soldiers along with women and children in Kilgoblin Castle; and the 117 soldiers hanged after the fall

56   Thomas Bartlett, 'War and society in Ireland, 1690-1760' in W.A.Maguire (ed), *Kings in conflict* (Belfast, 1990), pp. 173-84

57   *That great expedition for Ireland by way of underwriting proposed by both houses of parliament ... heere vindicated* (London, 1642): CUL, BC Hib. 7.642.99

of Ardmore Castle.[58] By 1646 this *de facto* policy had spread to England, and a parliamentary ordinance had decreed that 'no quarter shall henceforth be given to any Irishman or papist born in Ireland captured on sea or land'. Such orders were carried out: there was outrage when Captain Willougby's company of Irish (Protestant) royalists was pitched overboard after being intercepted at sea en route to fight for Charles I,[59] and after the fall of Shrewsbury, 13 Irish soldiers who had served in the royalist army in Ireland were taken out and hanged. In retaliation, Prince Rupert promptly hanged some Roundhead prisoners, and an agitated pamphlet controversy ensued, sharpened by Rupert's contention that the Irishmen executed were in fact English Protestant.[60] One pamphleteer helpfully suggested that a sure way to spot an Irishman, and thus avoid such unfortunate mistakes, was to ask him to say a word with an 'H' in it such as Smith or Faith: if he pronounced these words 'Smit' or 'Fait' then he would reveal his national origins.

Following the Williamite victory in Ireland in 1691, perhaps 20,000 Jacobite swordsmen were permitted, indeed encouraged, to take themselves off to the French and other armies, with the state even providing the necessary transports for that purpose. There was evident a firm determination to keep Irish Catholic recruits out of the king's armies: after all, given that Catholics (and particularly Irish Catholics) were associated with James II, it would have been madness to allow them to join the army in order, as one writer put it, 'to guard us from themselves'.[61] This prohibition was maintained well into the eighteenth century. Indeed, so determined were the military authorities to keep Irish Catholics out that they in effect banned all Irish from the ranks of the army, reasoning that the wily papists might pass themselves off as Protestants in order to join the colours. As is well-known, this bar on Irish Catholic recruitment proved difficult to police and because recruits of any sort were so difficult to come by, there were many instances of officers turning a blind eye to Catholic enlistments. But such practices were frowned upon, and if caught the culprits faced punishment. It appears to have been the demands of the Seven Years War (1756 - 63) that forced a reassessment of this policy of exclusion. The war was both

---

58 *A letter from an eminent person in the northern army ... also a letter concerning the Lord Inchequin* (London, 1648): CUL, BC Hib. 7.648.1; *True intelligence from Ireland* (London, 1642): CUL, BC Hib. 7.642.1/12; *A iournall of the most memorable passages in Ireland. Especially ... at Munster ... wherein is ... the siege of Ardmore Castle... with ... Liscarroll* (London, 1642): CUL, BC Hib. 7.642.48. For the British isles context of such killings see Charles Carlton, *Going to the wars: the experience of the British civil wars, 1638-1651* (London, 1992), pp. 33-8

59 *A declaration made by the rebels in Ireland against the English and Scottish protestants* (Waterford, 1645); CUL, BC Hib. 7.644.38

60 *A true and full relation of the manner of the taking of the citie and castle of Shrewsbury. With the conditions ...* (London, 1645): CUL, BC Hib. 7. 645.4 [The principal condition was that the Irish soldiers should 'be delivered up which we shall hang by authority']; Earl of Essex, *A letter from the earl of Essex to ... Prince Rupert concerning the putting to death of souldiers come out of Ireland ... with his highnesse's answer* (Bristol, 1645): CUL, BC Hib. 7.645.5

61 *Aphorisms relating to the kingdom of Ireland humbly submitted to the most noble assembly of the lords and commons at the great convention at Westminster* (London, 1689): CUL, BC Hib. 7.689.51

territorially extensive and manpower intensive and the need to garrison forts from India to Canada (and areas in between) forced a re-think. Recruitment began of those Scots Highlanders who a decade earlier had charged Cumberland's men at Culloden; and by the end of the war major proposals were on the table to recruit regiments of Irish Catholics. The outbreak of the War of American Independence gave a boost to those who sought to find in Ireland's Catholic population a solution to the manpower problems of the British Empire; but it was the commencement of war with France in 1793 that saw the wholesale open recruitment of Irish Catholics both into the regular army and navy, and into the Irish Militia. Not only were Irish Catholics encouraged to fight in the armed forces abroad but they were also expected to be the primary defence force within Ireland. Within a generation, the British state had gone from a policy of firm exclusion of Catholic soldiers to one of forced inclusion; from fear of Catholic numbers to reliance on them. The reasons for this reversal of a long-standing policy need not concern us: but it had major implications for the future of the Irish state, the development of Irish nationalism and the garrisoning of the British empire: in short, so far as Ireland was concerned, it may be that the mass recruitment of Irish Catholics into the armed forces of the crown - by the 1840s they constituted at least 40% of the rank and file of the Victorian army - constituted the key military revolution of the period 1600 to 1800.[62]

What conclusions can we draw from this discussion? We may say that seventeenth-century Ireland was a state shaped by war and by warriors, and that eighteenth-century Irish society displayed many signs of its martial past, in its apparent willingness to pay for large numbers of soldiers and in its worship of the uniform. In large measure, military activity on the island from the 1590s to the 1690s can be viewed in a context formed by the new European ideas and practices concerning warfare; certainly the students of the 'Academy of Warre' that was Ireland from the 1590s on proved adept at learning their trade and showed themselves to be able teachers in England and elsewhere. In addition, the growth of an Irish fiscal state underpinning a significant and sizeable military establishment from the late seventeenth century on fits in well with what historians of other countries have uncovered in their quest for the origins of other modern states. However, the ferocity with which civilians on all sides, and military prisoners in particular were treated in the Irish wars is disturbing, and puzzling. Perhaps the answer may lie in Ireland's anomalous position within the British state: part kingdom, part colony; and it may be that the ferocious and promiscuous nature of Irish warfare - at least up to the 1650s, but also in 1798 - may stem from its essentially colonial nature. In this respect, the

---

62 See in particular Terence Denman, 'Hibernia officina militum: Irish recruitment to the British regular army, 1660-1815' in *The Irish Sword*, vol. xx (no.80), pp. 148-166; Thomas Bartlett, '"A weapon of war yet untried:" Irish Catholics and the armed forces of the crown, 1760-1830' in Keith Jeffery and T. G. Fraser (ed) *Men, women and war* (Dublin, 1993), pp. 66-85

63 *The Irish Hudibras, or Fingallian Prince taken from the sixth book of Vergil's Aeneid and adapted to the present times* (London, 1689): CUL, BC Hib. 7.689.79

Indian wars in British North America in the seventeenth century might offer a valuable comparative perspective to the Irish military experience.

The Indians' 'skulking way of war' was clearly not all that different to what many English commanders saw as a native Irish predilection for ambushes from woods and bogs: 'The [Irish]', wrote one 'make it their business to find out steps and clumpers and practice the trotting therein with so much ease that like the wild Indians in their swamps and woods when they have committed any outrage or mischief, thither they betake themselves to a sanctuary and from thence are called bog-trotters'.[63] And when one writer in North America sought to explain for a London readership the nature of the terrain in which the Indian wars were being fought, he described how the Indians dwelled in a 'moorish place overgrown with woods and bushes but soft like a quagmire or Irish bogg over which horse cannot nor English foot (without great difficulty) passe'.[64]

This is a point of some importance. To avoid combat, to employ hit and run tactics, to kill from ambush and crucially then to have recourse to the woods and forests was seen as base and ignoble, as unEnglish, unchristian and finally as not human. With the enemy seen as savages and barbarians, closer to wolves and animals than to men - ('but one (if one) degree removed from unreasonable bruits' [sic])[65] - all ethical constraints on the conduct of war could be removed.[66] Hence the severed heads piled up outside Sir Humphrey Gilbert's tent, hence the scorched earth policy of Mountjoy, and hence the storms of Wexford and Drogheda, and other lesser atrocities. Hence also the refusal to categorise Irish conflicts as in fact war, at least until mid-century; and hence the routine execution of captured prisoners, for these were not soldiers but 'rebels' or 'inhuman wretches', or whatever. When Colonel Sir Frederick Hamilton on one of his punitive raids in north-west Ulster - raids which featured looting, burning, casual killing and beheadings - captured Charles McGuire ('the only best souldier and captain amongst them [the rebels]') he immediately ordered his execution. The injured McGuire was carried on a wheelbarrow to the gallows where he reportedly 'rayled at us all for that he could not obtain a souldier's death to be shot at a post having been twice ransomed in two king's services, France and Spain, and this morning commanding 300 proper men, not thinking that night to dye like a dogge on Manorhamilton's gallowes'.[67] Similarly when Sir Hardress Waller in a skirmish in 1642 recorded 600 rebel dead to one

---

64 Lepore, *The name of war*, p. 85: see also on this point James Axtell (ed) *The European and the Indian: essays in the ethno-history of North America* (Oxford, 1981) where he cites observers to the effect that Indian warfare was essentially unchristian because the Indians 'seldom or never dar[e] to meet our soldiers in the open field' and that 'every swamp is a castle to them [Indians]', pp. 140-1, 145

65 *A seasonable warning to Protestants...* (London, 1680): CUL, BC HIB. 7.680.14

66 See Patricia Palmer, *Language and conquest in early modern Ireland* (Cambridge, 2001) for a detailed treatment of this theme; 'Like brutish indians, these wylde Irish live/...cruel and bloody, barbarous and rude (cited, ibid., p. 21)

67 *Another extract of more letters sent out of Ireland, informing the condition of the Kingdom as it now stands* (n.p., 1643): CUL, BC Hib. 7.643.3

casualty on his own side, he reflected that 'this and the like strange victories ... do give us no small heart and courage amidst the great wants we now undergo in this now almost desolate country and makes our men go on with such incredible resolution as we reade of the old Romans amongst the barbarous nations';[68] and at Cloghnakilty, county Cork in 1643 'we found in the town not above twenty men, women and children which our troopers killed all, and ranged about and found some hundred more hid in gardens and killed all'.[69] Such incidents could be multiplied, and such actions and tactics were often replicated in the Indian wars of the seventeenth century where scorched earth tactics, burned villages and indiscriminate massacre were common.[70]

This is not however to say simply that the Irish were regarded and treated as Indians, and that Irish warfare was merely colonial warfare, for there were always those, as we have seen, who could see the quality of the Irish as trained soldiers, and there were always voices which recognised the common humanity in the Irish enemy. Our witness to the Cloghnakilty killings, for example, had a moment of doubt in his depiction of the carnage: 'there might you have seen every sex discovered and some lying on their backs, old, young, and none spared; at some sights I could have pitied but consider that pity spoyles a city, I durst not cherish that charity'.[71] Rather this view of the Irish as savages was one which was, I think, predominant in the early seventeenth century but which then was overtaken by a more benign view as the century wore on. Irish soldiers made their own contribution to this development: conscious of the low esteem in which they were held, the Irish graduates of the 'Academy of Warre' defined themselves, and other Irish, by their martial profession and their soldierly qualities. Gerat Barry in his *Discourse on Miltitary Discipline* bluntly described himself as Irish on the title page, and laid great emphasis on the role of the Irish in the latest battlefield tactics, siegecraft, and 'fireworkes' or explosives. In his earlier doctored account of the siege of Breda, he had also highlighted Irish courage under fire. Just as Geoffrey Keating was aware that an appropriate history would lift the Irish in the eyes of the world, so Barry was aware that the view of the Irishman as a professional soldier embarked in the 'noble profession of arms' was the perfect riposte to those who persisted in viewing the Irish as brutes, savages and barbarians.[72] As the century wore on, it was Barry's view that tended to prevail, with perhaps unlikely support from Oliver Cromwell - who went out of his way to pardon

---

68 *A true relation of the late occurrences in Ireland in two letters. One ... by ... Sir Hards Waller ...* (London, 1642): CUL, BC Hib. 7.642.109

69 *Good newes from Ireland: from Kimsale, Bandum, Clarakelty* [sic] ... (London, 1642): CUL, BC Hib. 7.642.47

70 See I.K Steele, *Warpaths: Invasions of North America* (Oxford, 1994); and Daniel K. Richter, *The ordeal of the Longhouse: the peoples of the Iroquois league in the era of European colonisation* (Chapel Hill, 1992)

71 *Good newes from Ireland,* op. cit.

72 For Barry's writings, see D.M.Rankin 'The art of war: military writing in Ireland in the mid-seventeenth century' (Oxford University unpublished D.Phil. thesis, 1999). For Keating's purpose see Bernadette Cunningham, *The world of Geoffrey Keating: history, myth and religion in seventeenth-century Ireland* (Dublin, 2000)

his opponent at Clonmel, Hugh Dubh O'Neill - and from Lord Orrery who did not view his opponents as savages and barbarians incapable of noble emotions.[73] By the time of the Jacobite war, despite determined efforts to recast that conflict as a re-run of the 1640s, those taking part grudgingly conceded that the enemy were in fact 'like us': 'They have a numerous army, their pretended king is at the head of them and all the kingdom is in their hands'.[74] It would be many decades before open recruiting of the Irish into the British army could take place, but this shift in perception - from savage to soldier - was vital to that process. The 'Academy of Warre' might prove to be the crucible of Irish identity in the early modern era.

Much of the research on which this lecture is based was undertaken while I was Parnell Fellow at Magdalene College Cambridge. My thanks to the Master, President and my fellow-Fellows of Magdalene for making my stay so enjoyable.

---

73 For Orrery see John Kerrigan, 'Orrery's Ireland and the British problem, 1641-79' in David J. Baker and Willy Maley (ed), *British identities and English renaissance literature* (Cambridge, 2002), pp. 197-225

74 [Earl of Halifax?], *The character of the Protestants of Ireland, impartially set forth in a letter, in answer to seven queries ...* (London, 1689): CUL, BC Hib. 7.689.54